ERIATA ORIBHABOR

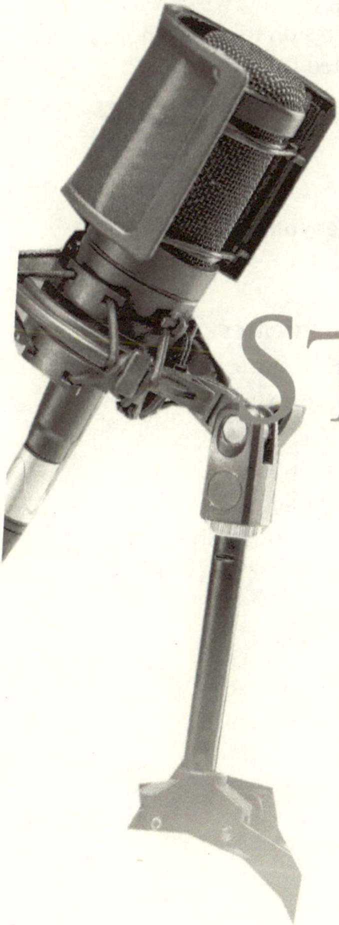

YOU HAVE THE STAGE

YOU HAVE THE STAGE

ISBN: 978-978-58113-3-9

Published by:
Something for Everybody Ventures (SFEV)

Plot 55 Basheer Augusto Street,
off Bode Thomas Road,
Surulere, Lagos, Nigeria

Tel: +2348100091760
Email: edbabor@gmail.com
Facebook: https://web.facebook.com/oribhabor
Website: www.naijapidginworldwide.com

Product of SFEV, Nigeria

COMMENTS

Eriata knows how to knit words with well-tailored lines that capture one's mind. On a canvas of words, he is the acrylic that lingers long after an artwork dries up. In this wholesome piece, he takes one on a roller coaster of memories unfolding real life scenarios. Sometimes I just want to read yet I can't help but recite. One would love to regurgitate. I love that he peels the layers off Naija's secret and impounds them in his pieces. Relatable, and straight to the point. He is well versed with stroking one's heart to a dance. He invades the psyche and serenades one with poetry in its basic and complex forms. His poems are reflective and cut across all spheres of human endeavors - humour, sadness, anger, politics, humanity, sanity, societal ills etc. A whole meal not just to nibble on as they leave indelible imprints in your mind's eye. I recommend it highly. He is deserving of an applause for configuring poetry into a medium of utmost expression with an audacious aura unapologetic about airing his views.

Michelle Nnanyelugo
Spoken word poet
NkwelleEzunaka, Anambra State

YOU HAVE THE STAGE is an excellent content parceled with examples from real life happenings, delivered with skillful use of first person sources, showcasing some excesses of performing ACTS especially as it chronicles stage presence, sense of self, timing and the backstage drills. Herein, readers take cues on practical suggestions to improve on individualistic approach to stage arts.

The construction of the book in parts fit into a thrilling memoir of the author's analysis of various settings that breathe life into the core theme explored. Also, it reflects genuine appreciation for the art of writing via the spoken call bit. Cultural appraisal comes in through the choice of Naija Pidgin in the other segment of spoken call. Do you wish to spill the truth about societal ills? The spoken call lines will make you yearn for the stage. All pages are creatively stringed to inform the reader and ignite positiveness towards birthing responsible artists. The spoken call lines are both entertaining and informing. On the overall, the style of the book is one of a kind and the transition from one point to the next will make you read for hours seamlessly. This is worth everyone's read!

Adekunle - OguntoyinboPhebian
Performance Poet, Lagos, Nigeria

FOREWORD

Now I have the stage - or should I say the page?

The title of this book is energizing. It recalls a myriad of images of lights flashing, smoke oozing from smoke machines, bodies in tight black leather gyrating to the spirits of sounds blaring from speakers on stage corners, microphones cradled in crooks of sweaty arms clad in dazzling attire to the maddening of a young crowd lost in the haze of life played at a dizzying degree of speed.

Or, a barrage of words spitting slowly, dropping tongues of flames, baptizing the cafe in a rain of emotions, encapsulated in simple words that bear the life of a poet. Now you have the stage. Now I have the page. And I'm inspired to bring the fire I usually would reserve for a stage and a live mic to this page because the title inspires me to reminisce on days and seasons of burning words dripping from my lips.

Eriata has conceptualised a phenomenon. The phenomenon of the stage - the sphere of intense and virile expression of all that's human, he captures the idea and wraps it in this slim volume for enlightenmentof those who don't deem to show the reverence any great artiste and performer has had to revel in to be honoured by the stage, it's purveyors and those who drink in its magic.

The stage like Eriata espouses is a hallowed ground. The stage is a mirror. The stage is a school. The stage is a shrine. The stage is a playground. The stage is life in motion, in expression, in thought, in postulation.

Now You Have the Stage has successfuly transformed the page into a stage in the same way performers have taken the magic of words buried in the pages of great books to the stage and breathed a new life into it.

What I like about this book is its coaching and wisdom for new purveyors of the art of performance and the knowledge they need to have. But much more than that, it proceeds to unveil a hybrid of spoken word and clarion call with the written literature of social change and development. The power of the various mediums are well represented and as you read you visualize the performance or the calling that would ensue in a live portrayal of the script.

And then there's the pidgin. His mastery and ease of delivery in Naijapidgin rivals his ability to pontificate in proper English - it surpasses it with the fluidity of his poetry. I have often wondered how to write and recite poetry in pidgin. I guess I need not search too far for an example.

This book is a blitzkrieg. It is militant. It is quick. It hits its target. And it is incisive.

Sage S Hassan
Poet/Writer/Life Coach
Lagos, Nigeria

CONTENTS

Part One

YOU HAVE THE STAGE

THE STAGE

You have the stage to read a poem. In five minutes, you told its history and highlighted its benefits to your audience. Indulgence of the audience was stretched to breaking-point limit. It took you less than a minute to read the poem. What did you just do to a patient and understanding audience?

* Next time you are asked to read a poem on stage, please introduce yourself and the poem's title and go ahead to read it. You don't have to tell its story before reading it. Just go ahead and read. Let the audience relish every line of the poem. On popular demand, you may be called back to read same poem.

* Similarly, you may not have introduced the poem but giving a lecture after reading is unnecessary except the audience overwhelmingly called for it. However, you may politely request to say something about the poem.

* In case you are being specially hosted as an author, you may take the liberty of doing whatever on stage but caution must be applied to avoid putting up attitudes that may amount to abusing the sensibility of your audience.

You have the stage to present a poem in the popular spoken word pattern. Rather than introduced yourself and the poem, you first did an "introductory rigmarole" thinking it has a way of adding up to the beauty of your presentation. Apart from eating up the time allotted to you, you annoy others on queue. How would you want the audience to perceive you? What did you do to your name?

It's an OPEN MIC session and your turn to mount the stage came, you felt "too big" to stick to the rule of one poem per poet and went ahead to do two to the chagrin of the event anchor. Just when the anchor was to move up stage to take the mic from you, you went ahead with a third performance. How would you want to be perceived? If others before you behaved in like manner, what would be the chances of you coming on stage? What about a line-up of others itching to have the stage? Please note the followings:

* The stage is an opportunity that could make or mar the fortunes of any one.
* Never take any audience for granted.
* Be apt.
* Don't abuse the rules/guidelines set by event organisers who originally set the stage.
*Never assume that your popularity cuts across all locations and be demoralized when not hyped before coming up stage.
*Learn to personally prime yourself for the stage.
* A landmark outing is better than ten 'stage rigmaroles' or 'patch-ups' being forced down the throat of an audience.
*Always allow the audience to be.

BACKSTAGE

Every stage has a backstage determining its overall setting of sound, colour and beauty. Back stages are constituted by what we popularly refer to as 'behind the scenes activities' that go a long way in preparing the stage and all that happen on it. When you attend an event that was painstakingly planned and studiously delivered, you enjoy seamless flow of scenes from beginning to the end.

Replete are examples of events I had attended and never wanted the show to come to an end. Last year, I had the privilege of attending Simply Poetry's "Night of the Spoken Word" (NSW) in Abuja entitled; Man Made Gods. It was more of a one-man (almost 2hrs) performance by Dike Chukwumerije. So gripping was the event, that the audience were wrapped in educative entertainment never wanting an end. When it did end, it took Dike Chukwumerije a 'special announcement' for I and others to begin considering whether to leave the hall or not. But as Nigerians, we are used to finding ways of being busy. In our minds, the show shouldn't have ended at the time it did. To keep it going at other fronts, we indulged in unplanned photo sessions inside the Merit Hall, Abuja venue of the event.

The 2018 edition Feast of Words organised by Samson IruesiriKukogho's Word Rhymes and Rhythms (WRR) and Poets in Nigeria's The ArtHub, Lagos respectively also came out splendid. I remember seeing a huge number of members of the audience milling around after both events had ended - they wanted more of creativity served as packs of alluring gifts.

It is very important that events are well planned and intelligently prosecuted. From time to time, successes made of such events, should be built upon as mark of seriousness and determination for progress and development. A good example of an event that keeps growing in the face of lack of sponsorship is Festival Poetry Calabar (FPC) started by few poets at the Marina Resort, Calabar in 2015. The 2018 edition of the festival was way better, bigger and bolder as promised by the organisers - Poets in Nigeria Initiative. The Local Organising Committee led by Mr. Bassey Asuquo had support from members and volunteers: VeralynChinenye, Ask'YahOtonte, NkanuGabriell, Isaac Daniel, Blessing Sam, Hilda Ojong, Chinatu Blessed Orji, Utibe Eno Ekpuk, Riches Solomon, Elizabeth Ita, Felix Ayuk, Dorcas Odok, Rebecca KakongMonity, etc. The promise is to keep strengthening the festival's 'back stages' for a much more successful FPC's stage 2019.

As individuals, we have respective areas of strengths and weaknesses. Personally, identifying one's strength can be tricky. Most times, it takes associating with others to spot exactly what one could do or better still, truly appreciating the 'you in oneself'. Against this background, the stage goes beyond the physical stage - the one who witnessed a performance on a stage and gets inspired by it must have had a feel of it. Therefore, the physical stage was first built in the subconscious - herein lies creativity.
The following questions may agitate the average reader of thinking the way forward for whatever event one may be organising. Also, it will help anyone in an audience to read between the lines while appreciating whatever event being attended or to be attended. Why are some events full of sound and little to offer? Why are some events heavily bolstered by lots of stage effects such as lighting without much to deliver in terms of content? The stage is a combination of creations from the inside of us before they manifest as performances on stage. Every audience wants a good show determined by several variables and careful planning is key.

I have always advocated for careful planning, giving a reasonable time frame between planning, promotion of the event and the event proper - also referred as 'period of gestation.' Sometimes, we have ample time to plan but prefer 'last minutes arrangements' believing that, we will make it. 'Last minute people' are those who are ever ready with failure excuses to tender. If you ever attended an event where the organisers tell the audience reason (s) why "A" wasn't 'B" or why a "D" had to join a team a day before the show, it doesn't speak well for the group. It was better the audience be left to make deductions and live with them whilst looking forward to the next show/performance. This brings me to a theatre performance I attended last year December, at the Cultural Centre in Calabar. Without gainsaying, I watched an action movie on stage. I was so impressed that I started thinking of how to meet with any member of the cast for possible 'sign on.' When it was time for the entire cast to do the traditional bye to the audience, the producer stated that, what was performed on stage was rehearsed in 15 days. Unknown to him, his comment was an anti-climax for an event that was fittingly climaxed with palpable sense of enjoyment. At this juncture, I began to harbour a feeling that I wasn't given what was my due. Meaning, the performance should have been better? If I had paid to watch it, I should be asking for a refund, or so it seems.

CONCEPT AND PERCEPTION

Concept and perception of stage and the totality of what it represents is everything good. Apprised from the point of extremes, it's scaled higher than good - if anything, it's perfect; a veiled allusion to the value, deserving of every stage.

A popular cliché in political circles holds that, "every country gets the leadership she deserves" - same with the stage. Every community gets the stage or stages she deserves. How we build, use and manage our stages go a long way in the perception others may form or hold of us. A lot could be read/said about a people's history, culture and tradition via events that hold on her stages. If stages are humans, they can't be stooges - never would they be associated with 'anything goes.' They are platforms showcasing the finest of things - a boiling hub of creativity that's routinely honed and developed. The more one is exposed to the stage, the more one builds needed confidence to speak on any topic.

The overall outlook of a stage is a selling point that every audience should be enchanted by. In popular parlance, this is called 'packaging.' Thus, the stage should always be viewed from positive standpoints of hard work and awesome deliveries.

As earlier stated, while the stage was first built in the subconscious of her builders, it is appropriate looking at it beyond raised up platforms commonly found in theatre/event halls. Whether built up or a normal flat ground, once a space is designated as where one should either speak/read/make a presentation, it is a stage that should be accorded its pride of place.
Whoever mounts the stage should have the undivided attention of the audience. The content and character of every audience is judged by the way it treats the stage. Maltreatment of any one on stage is an abuse of the stage which is bigger than the individual availing himself/herself

of it. Whoever is reading/speaking/performing on any stage, should be seen or perceived as one deserving of every necessary regard. It is against this background that, members of any audience are expected to freely offer claps of encouragement or finger clicks to whoever is to either mount the stage, on the stage or may have just concluded its usage. Friendly audiences are judged by the way they handle whoever mounts the stage. Considering this, a raucous audience is most likely going to be adjudged as disrespectful to the stage no matter what may have happened on it. There are situations where the one on stage deserves being booed out but respect for the stage should discourage such an action. A clap of appreciation is always needed.

YOU AND THE AUDIENCE

If stages are humans, they are ambassadors of people and places. Simply put, they are image-making tools that every community should go for. The kind of attention a people place on her stage is the level of rating for her future, weaved around paths to engendering creativity.

Every stage is an opportunity waiting to be unleashed. Having the stage for a minute could change anyone's fortune for good. As a member of the NNPC Junior Staff Club (Saipem Camp), Ekpan, Warri many years ago, I was opportune to air my views on furthering the fortunes of the club during a pre-election meeting. When it was time for elections into various club management positions, I was surprisingly nominated and elected as the Publicity Secretary. I needed no one to tell me that what happened was a case of stage well utilised. How else would one easily land an executive position of a club of that status when I never campaigned for it? The singular opportunity of speaking to the people for a few minutes was the magic.

Like everything in life, the stage could also be the undoing of anyone. That lots of people dread the stage is incontestably true. I had witnessed situations where people earmarked to speak on assigned topics on stage pleaded for others to represent them. This is not saying that whoever asked another to represent him/her at an event where he/she was billed to speak did so out of fear of the stage. No. However, one may not be wrong to say, the fear of the stage is the beginning of wisdom. The wisdom of seeing the stage as a friendly ally is an encouragement any day. People with the later disposition do mount the stage with confidence believing that, no matter the circumstance, the outcome of associating with the stage would be positive.

Whatever one does on a stage is meant to either showcase or promote whatever for higher endeavours. The more imposing a stage is, the more frightening it appears. In reverse, the level of back stage preparedness given to any stage, determines how much most people are motivated to want to mount it. Despite backstage preparations and readiness, some who mounted stages ended up embarrassing themselves. Don't blame them. The stage has a touch of sacredness that only regular stage users would decode. What are codes necessary for stage users?

1. Be well versed in the subject matter to be presented.
2. Have enough back-stage preparation
3. Be confident
4. No display of overconfidence

5. Be humble
6. Have capacity to turn water to wine
7. Be appreciative of content and character of the audience

BOOK STAGES

Beyond the traditional built up stages that are prepared for speakers/presenters and performances in any name, pages are stages. From pages, authors/poets/writers speak to readers just like we experience on physical stages. From pages, people are enlightened and connected to greater endeavours. In view of this, the author should be perceived as one 'standing' on his book (stage): addressing his readers (audience). In this case the stage is not within walls but beyond traditional stages found in walled buildings or open theatres.

Until the coming of the Internet, physical stages were limited by the number of people that could use it and audiences whose numbers were also limited by space. In reverse, the hugeness of books as stages is not space defined and the number of people who may meet a book is indeterminable. In this regard, it's indubitably true that the coming of internet/online book downloads, is also strategic to the promotion of books as stages, and central to the development of physical stages beyond walls as mentioned.

As stated earlier, every stage enjoys a backstage where everything about what comes on it should be painstakingly prepared. Every well-prepared book must have passed through the eyes of others or editors. Collectively put, readers of any book belong to her expanding audience.

While producers and directors work behind the scenes to have the best of what comes onstages, authors employ editors to avoid mistakes/flops in their books, which are also stages. Except for events like special guest author readings where authors are hosted to read from their works, the author may never have the privilege of speaking about his/her book and its subject matter. This is unlike regular stages where the one having the stage could respond to enquiries from members of the audience. However, with the coming of internet, authors could speak to readers/followers in far flung places.

The role of books to people and society cannot be overemphasized because the one with a book has a stage upon which bigger stages could be built.

THE AGREEMENT

When we first build stages in our heads for either books or regular/physical stages, we yearn for perfection in all. Having for the umpteenth time said this, it is appropriate to state that stage builders are thinkers whose passion for critical paths to successes cannot be questioned. Stage builders are not seekers of short cuts to delivering on the ultimate purpose of societal good. Once the need to build a stage in any form is identified, naming it comes next viz: titles, sub-titles and ultimately the main title that everyone comes to associate with. Therefore, various titles are mini-stages that sum up to what we all come to know as the stage/stages.

Titling or naming is a necessary step that serves as guide and inspiration to every builder requiring focus on the ultimate good of any project. Naming doesn't equate success. We have seen beautiful titles or creatively packaged stages, which ultimately didn't meet the expectations of audiences (readers - in case of books) or physical halls. Every naming speaks for itself as determined by authors of books or stage directors and producers. This takes us back to stages and all that either transpired or would transpire. Although, we have subjective assessments to make about respective books, we will agree that the content of a book is never judged by its cover. This is also true of a physical stage.

Having the stage is having the world on one's palm. Lending stages their desired credence, amounts to respect for performers or whoever may use the stage. Against this background, it is always important to properly spell out 'ways to go' for everyone that has something to do with whoever and whatever would be coming up stage. By this, I mean reaching an agreement on who gets what, be it financial or otherwise. For example, if the one in charge of a physical backstage compromises on standards, the stage's quality/output would be affected (physical or book stages). When performers are compelled to spare a day or two to rehearse in preparation for the stage, it is to serve the audience the best. All cards must therefore be put in the open for everyone to agree before stage users mount the stage. Whether the audience noticed it or not, members of the cast would say for sure how the entire performance would have been if a key member of the cast was on stage. Same for books hurriedly taken to the press without due diligence of editing or advice on the 'way to go.'

THEARTRE EXPERIENCE, CREATIVE ECONOMY

Every stage births a theatre experience and offers opportunities for showcasing a peoples' creative parts for socio-economic wellbeing. A visit to the National Theatre in Iganmu, Lagos would open one's eyes to the beauty of arts in diversity. The first thing that comes to mind is, if the space could be accorded its rightful place for art and tourism, it would be one of the nation's busiest tourism destinations. In line with the vision of making tourism, hospitality, entertainment and sports the centrepiece of development agenda in Lagos state, Governor AkinwumiAmbode recently commissioned Lagos Theatre at Oregun, Lagos. According to the governor, this would be replicated at Igando, Epe and Badagry areas of Lagos respectively. This is to 'expand arts and performance spaces in Lagos and promote a thriving creative economy within the communities where these projects are located'. The 400-capacity hall, has amongst others, artiste changing rooms, rehearsal hall, restaurant space, rest rooms, alternative power generating sets and well laid out car parks.

The positive impact of the mentioned initiative on the youth of various communities where they are located would be judged against positive enlightenment and enjoyment and the possibility of honing and promoting their artistic prowess. This can also be looked at via prisms of peace and harmonious living.

The stage experience and benefits therefore cuts beyond tribe, religion and what have you. In view of that, a stage's neutrality shows in various activities that take place on it; same for books that could fall in the hands of anyone, leaving trails of positive impacts.

=Part Two=

THE SPOKEN CALL

(Anthology of written calls to action)

INTRODUCTION

Spoken Calls are calls to action crafted to sensitize presenters, readers and listeners to societal ills whilst proffering a way forward for the good of all. It's a term coined by the author, Eriata Oribhabor, who wrote the first ever Spoken Call entitled *Sokoto in your Shokoto*presented on stage by different poets who registered to participate in a maiden Spoken Call presentation/performance contest which held at The ArtHub, Surulere, Lagos, Nigeria on 15th August, 2015.

At the second edition of The ArtHub, Surulere, Lagos, in October 2015, a Spoken Call entitled *Today is Independence* written by the author was presented.

The third and fourth editions of The ArtHub held at Natives Hospitality Restaurant, Victoria Island, Lagos and Oaks Garden Cultural Centre, Isheri, Igando, Lagos respectively without the presentation of a Spoken Call.

However, the fifth edition of ArtHub witnessed the presentation of a spoken call entitled *Mr Clement* also written by the author. The event was held on 6th of October 2018 at Oaks Garden Cultural Centre, Isheri, Olofin, Lagos.

While appreciating everyone who participated in the mentioned Spoken Call presentations/events, it is important stating that this collection of spoken calls is to expose readers to the history of spoken calls in Nigeria whilst encouraging calls to positive actions for societal advancement.

In addition, it practically illustrates the importance of both the book and physical stages in delivering pungent missives to humanity. Apart from the mentioned Spoken Calls, other Calls have never been presented/performed on stage before going to press but found worthy of making this anthology.

The place of the stage would be further appreciated as we delve into the world of presentations for positive reorientation and actions. Spoken calls in this collection were purposely written for the stage. Each one could be presented by a poet or a collaboration of poets. It is hoped that, they will further stimulate interests for presentation of uniquely written poems whose impact would reorient perspectives for creative reasoning and predisposition to securing the best from people and the authorities.

SPOKEN CALL EXPLAINED

A Spoken Call is a work of prose or poetry carefully worded to address burning societal ills with embedded solutions for a way forward. The first Spoken Call ever staged is entitled; Sokoto in your "Shokoto" written by Eriata Oribhabor and presented in a slam format.

While some say it was a poem, there are others who say it was a prose work. Whatever the conclusions, it was a Spoken Call dedicated to addressing burning questions to positively shape perspectives.

I am personally excited that what came as an idea, was made to hit the ground running with intelligent Spoken Word Poets and Artists who did justice to it. Thus, making history as the first set of participants at a Spoken Call event sure to grow bigger.

SOKOTO IN YOUR 'SHOKOTO'

This is a wake-up call flying with questions and solutions. How is your home performing? Where is the place of foreign in the scheme of things? How are you managing your local spaces? Is everything foreign bad? Is everything local good? How do you feel compromising your positive cultural values on the altar of selfishness? What do you gain damaging the core of the essence of your uniqueness?

Yesterday may have attempted a snatch of today but I laugh at anyone addressing the state-of-affairs in my state like one with water in his mouth.

I have some pleasing words for you; let none pound your ears with forlorn promises nor bathe you with lectures on anti-imperialism lacking verve of reckoning in today's global world, warming its heart to us. We may commune on pages of papers whilst speaking same language but knowing how much we lag in baggage of self-infliction matters.

Globalization may have many faces; let's face the one with a face that attunes with our place.

Slave trade once had a vibrant market in our land. Unfortunately, its vestiges still adorn the streets of our hearts but must be consigned to the past. Experiences therefrom, should be used as tools of inspiration...not despondency.

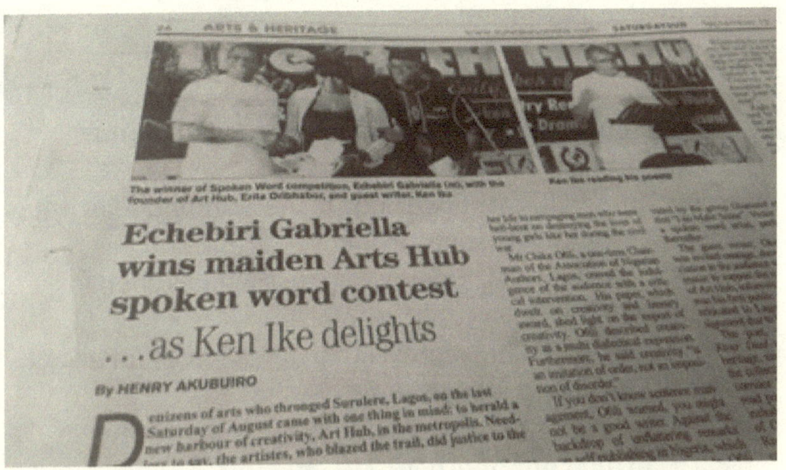

The winner of Spoken Word competition, Echebiri Gabriella (m), with the founder of Art Hub, Erita Oribhabor, and guest writer, Ken Ike

Echebiri Gabriella wins maiden Arts Hub spoken word contest

...as Ken Ike delights

By HENRY AKUBUIRO

Denizens of arts who thronged Surulere, Lagos, on the last Saturday of August came with one thing in mind: to herald a new harbour of creativity, Art Hub, in the metropolis. Needless to say, the artistes, who blazed the trail, did justice to the

I have some pertinent questions for you:

- When last did you see a functional local authority?
- Why can't we fix our drains?
- Why do we sign MoUs to be dumped in senseless lagoons?
- Who plucked our reasoning faculties?
- Why do we wash in sentimental tales of white, black, purple or green excuses?
- Has corruption a colour?
- Is environmental abuse not environmental abuse?

Search your consciences...
What's the colour of ineptitude? What is the taste of religious sentiment? Are these condiments for a healthy broth? What is tribal sentiment? Does it sound like one of the pillars of love to be embraced? If leaders revel in sentiments, would they ever climb above the walls of evil and ineptitude?

This is a wake-up call meant to pierce-deep consciences. Let's tell ourselves the truth and hit the ground running for justice and equity.

- Do most of our leaders know what leadership represents?
- Can't we judge them from how they manage our natural endowments?
- Is Human Rights not a book leaders should read but not swallow its contents hook, line and sinker?
- Shouldn't leaders choose and use what is good for their respective systems?
- Do you know how much our leaders have mortgaged our future for selfish ends?
- Won't we rather take to the streets against thieves than fight one another?
- Shouldn't those pillaging our collective till cool off behind bars?
- Isn't a flagrant denouncement of anything foreign escapism?

Let's ponder over key government establishments.

- Ever heard of the National Orientation Agency?
- What about the Council for Arts and Culture at the Federal and state levels?
- When last did you hear of the National Library of Nigeria?

The last time I visited one of their branches, I wept.
The time to come back home to ourselves and sound bold steps of our forebears who stood for truth and justice not winking, is now.
Reasons for our woes are within and solutions to our madness reside here. If politics should provide the much needed societal good, the goodness in us must blossom in the politics we display.

This is a wake-up call!

If in your opinions the above hasn't addressed touching questions and proffered solutions, go ahead and swallow the questions.

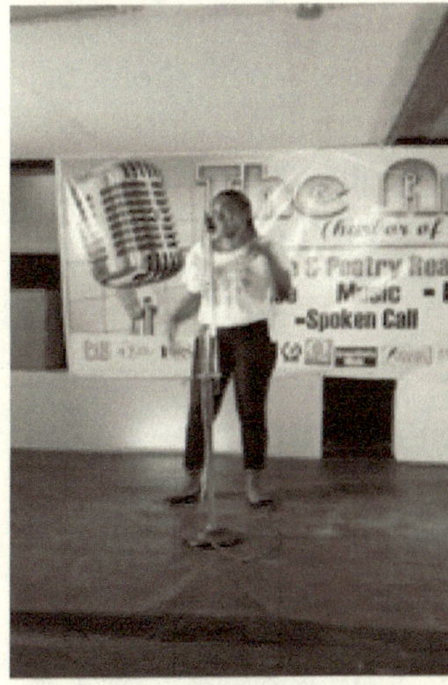

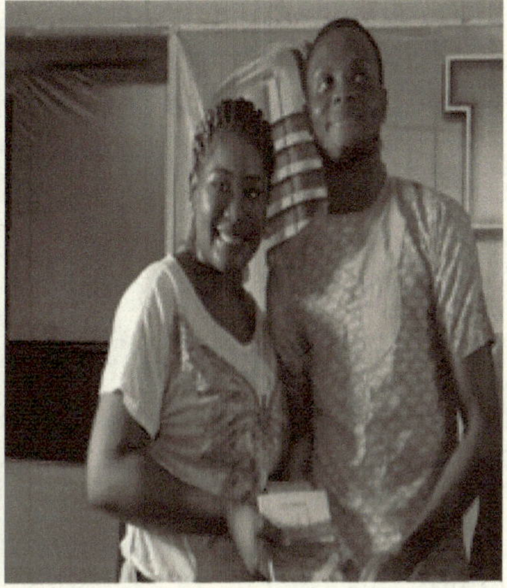

(B) Winner of the maiden edition of Spoken Call:
Echebiri Gabriella Imelda hands over the "baton" to the emerging winner of the second edition **Paul Word**
(A) Echebiri Imelda Gabriella - Winner, Maiden edition of Spoken Call
"Sokoto in your Shokoto" – (Naija pidgin): something one has but goes about in search for it.

TODAY IS INDEPENDENCE

Today is independence!

Mr. President will shake hands with Senate and the House for a new fragrance to take the air. Leaders will speak of heroes' past. Parks and gardens will go green, white and green. Its giver may have a honourable mention as a rendition of the Master's hand across the land.

Today is Independence!

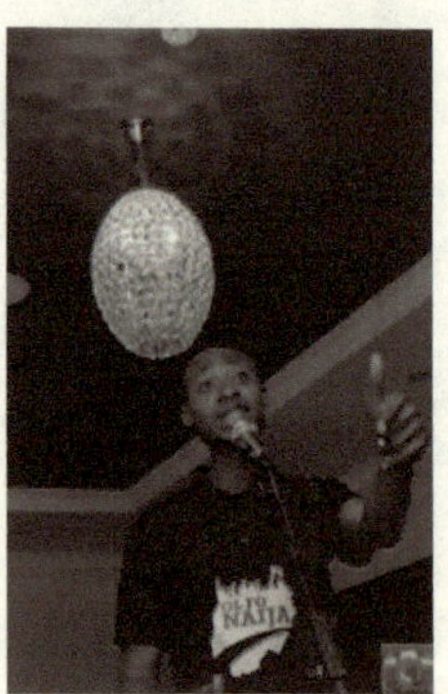

Flags of green and white will seize uncommon spaces, colonial wigs will mimic order, Frogs will jump with pomp and candour. God sons and god daughters will wash with tales of virtues, valour and recipes of freedom. Faded photos of the 60s will stand atop in all for coated freedom.

Today is independence!

What did you glean from photos splashed on billboard and flyers? God-given faces or imported hair? Well-cut lawns or dirty pawns? Neat open spaces and squares or gaping drains and beggars? Touristic stamps of hospitality or street hawkers of shame?
Order as right or madness? Questions of Malfeasance!

Today is independence!

Plastic smiles speak of sordid times...and celebration of wasted years...Where is the ground to shed our tears? Our fears may know no bound...our hopes may lie in sounds and rhythms of old. We must post these lines in bold fonts. We must front them on all fronts.

Today is independence!

A celebration of gains or pain? Tell them to stand again to gain the past... Tell them to reverberate in rated ways...
If meanings must celebration pride, our pride and essence must return from lost depths.

Today is independence!

What sense? What essence?

CELEBRATION OF MR CLEMENT

Welcome to my world of spoken calls. Today, we shall be talking about us and colours of weathering weathers. We shall embark on sniffing rides of tasty realities. We shall ruminate on risks of staying in the house of our houses, surviving the times. We shall look at power and the place of Mr. Clement in bettering the fortunes of our weathers. Finally, we shall talk about change in changing times.

The weather has been terribly hot, and Mr. Clement is repeatedly mentioned as responsible. Those in love with him are saying, this wouldn't be the first-time people would be denied weather rights and that, there shouldn't be cause for alarm. Similarly, some are openly saying most of us are outright lazy. In their words, "weather or no weather", one has to be "smart" like them, acquiring spaces for weather changes. I wasn't brought up that way. I want to earn all I have.

News making the round says, Mr. Clement has travelled to China for talks on sparkling weather investment for his people...Who doesn't know that traveling is a pastime; refreshing and rewarding?

Whoever says traveling is educating is dead right. A trip or two outside one's vicinity is always fantastic. Trips to first worlds are ever pleasant. Have you ever pondered where we belong? Can you tell how we came down this low? What world do we belong? A First world? Not a Second world... Hmmmm...We used to be a glorified third world - certainly not any more. Now a fourth world? No! Not a Fifth world...

It was interesting meeting some great friends who joked about our hallowed chambers of recurring craziness. Relieving how they were entertained by "monkeys", they laughed. I emphatically argued that, 'huuumans' not "monkeys" hold privileged positions in "our world." We argued and laughed with drums of rising argument that seemed to be climbing the roof tops.

Ladies and gentlemen, welcome to our world of jungle arenas...I am not talking about filth eating up our spaces. I am not mentioning the newness of street madness and open thievery. When you hear bells ring, don't they offer sounds, likened to that given by stones thrown to test the waters of good or bad? I have no story to tell. Ladiesand gentlemen let's go back to the past and win back honours. Let's eliminate shames of dogged games.

Like bees, let's be sincerely genuine. My people! My people!!

Thisspoken callis meant to put us on edges for creative bents forward.

I am neither *going nor coming* for politics. I am here to speak to your consciences.

WHAT'S THE NAME OF YOUR NATIONALISM?

You may have been born and raised in either Benin-city, Kano, Enugu or any other town in a colonially foisted Nigeria and never been to Warri, Maiduguri, Lagos, Abuja or any other place within its spheres but gunning to be a Senator. What kind of Senator wouldn't you be?

Tell me...

You have never travelled outside your place of birth, maturity abides by the day, dreams you dreamed are dreams you are dreaming. What won't the colour of your humanity be?

Tell me...

The last time you wanted to know other sides of your country, your parents said, you will be welcomed by human parts served on tables as meals. You are trapped in a world not knowing worlds within your world. What parental postulations wouldn't you debunk?

Tell me...

You are a brainwash of European and American mixes salted by contents of Arabic and Chinese calculations who proudly say; "I am Christian" or "I am Muslim." What space would you ever boast?

Tell me...

Your backyards are being systematically overrun by foreign intruders welcomed with open arms, they live with you and know your ways. Now they poke guns in your eyes. What country are you not building?

Tell me...

You are promoting drum beats of your locality, never have you raised your nation's flag. You walk spaces with conquering spirit of destruction, bent on taking over every available space and your heart resides across the borders. What's the name of your nationalism?

Tell me...

PEOPLE, MADNESS AND DEATHS

While our world spiral-drown in Borno state, many believed that, only in Afghanistan would such happen. Thus, stark realities were being handled with kid gloves. When sordid happenings began to play out in Adamawa and Taraba states, they were neither accorded serious attention nor deserved reportage in the national media. Upon flash arrivals in Kogi, Delta and Enugu states, the capacity of these unwholesome developments to cut holes deep enough to swallow a people and nation was downplayed. *Silence was the word.*

While the state of Plateau was being dismembered in phases of calculated killings, people and heritages were wiped out in Kaduna state, yet to recover from a history of repeated attacks and killings of mindless proportions. When the state of Benue was visited by madness and deaths, the case of Plateau was a child's play. That women were raped and burnt to death in the bushes of Edo and Delta states was something many of us thought would never happen in our world. When the IDP camps of Nasarawa state began to overflow with displaced people, madness and deaths made deep statements for all to grapple with. *Silence was the word.*

When a petrol laden tanker was reported to have turned over and busted into flames in the nation's most disorderly city Lagos, stench of burnt humans and property hovered her chaotic sphere. Revisited with mayhem never in our history known, Jos, the capital of plateau state was blood. A nation in pain and confusion tearfully renders daily songs of death. Partisan politicians warm up for elections with careless abandon. *Silence is the word.*

If terrorism is a 'foreign creature' that shouldn't be mentioned in our land, what's tearing down homes and communities? Why do farm lands reek of blood? If mentioning terrorism by its name isn't Nigerian, is it American or European? Or, the Arab strapped with thorns of death around his waist? If terrorism is neither a Book nor a Haram, will calling it Fulani Herdsmen make it fly? Will naming it Libya or Cattle Rustlers make it smile at us? If it never visited Bornu, Yobe, Zamfara, Adamawa, Taraba, Enugu, Edo, Delta and Benue states, it was never in A G A T U. If we say terrorism isn't here in our land, *Silence is the word.*

UP NAIJA!

Nigeria is winning this game. Medals in Borno. Goals in Zamfara. Heart rendering surprises in Benue, Plateau, Delta, Edo, Kogi, Adamawa, Taraba, Enugu and more...

Nigeria is technically superior. Book Haram is technically defeated. Bandits are technically checkmated. Herdsmen are technically sorted. Air, land and water are GPRS protected.

Nigeria is the heart beat of Africa. The biggest black nation in the world. The world looks up to her. She is potentially great. Her first name is POTENTIAL. She is alive all year round.

Nigeria is free from ritualism and kidnapping. One of her safest roads; Abuja - Kaduna Expressway is no more a beehive of criminality. Peace and tourism are celebrated on newspapers and TV screens. A road map for tourism will be relaunched in South Africa.

Nigeria's image is ever rising abroad. Her citizens are lively shoppers. Every supermarket respects them. They are household names in Indonesia. Americans love them. Europeans can't do without them.

Nigeria has the highest number of doctors in Africa. Many are finding their feet abroad. The meaning of health care gains ground by the day. Health tourism is a big business. India, China, Israel and Dubai are premium destinations.

Nigeria will rule space in 2020. Launching into Saturn isn't a problem because no Jupiter can stop it. The Chinese are ready. They are her biggest friend well-disposed to buy up countries willing to trade off their all.

Nigeria in space is bye to her energy problems. Her industries will bounce back with loudest of sounds. Agriculture will only be practically taught from space. No BOKO or HARAM can stop her.

Nigeria is a world power. World powers laugh at her big-for-nothing attitude. Her powers litter countries around the world. Naija is a study case of history.

FOR LAGOS

...flip not the bras tags, tag not with laggards in Lagos of rags and riches, grow beyond the nags to make it whole in this land.

Las las

pipul go be pipul of Lag
di Lasgidi of Naija
where pidgin nawota
wey no get enemy.
...inside this maddening box are "out-of-the -box" loads -
Lagos of mock boxers
who pleasure in boxing on streets of sensibilities.

Las las

pipulwey get time to wait
go see how blow
and blow dey fight for air
but no fight go happen.

...in this hell of a crazy place, insanity wears the face of sanity, sanity battles to survive insanity, a story many don't want to hear, it's still a hub that many die for a share.

Las las

population dey rise,
everybody dey pocket im shoulder
community living deh for here
one man fear na community fear.
...beautiful beaches and beach rats, "agberos" and street lords, "omoniles" and land speculators, "abegis" and sounds of rising lounges, "LASTMA and plenty madness.

Las las

every noise get im own music
dirty get im own perfume
LASTMA na pocket lawyer
99-standing, 44-sitting still deh
pipulweydeh, seydem go still deh.

Let's go back in one accord, stringing chords of creative whips, whip back thoughts for best shots, find reasons for worthy rewinds, flashback for cool throwbacks, riding the back of beauties we would gladly wave...

Let's play the travel game, naming names in names of places happily consumed, paint exciting captures of unforgettable reels that thrill, walk the work of their feels, planting seeds for humanity's good...

Let's sing songs off our poems, drum meanings of home they bear, invade palaces and places of mattered squares, dance as natives with eyes for international arenas, proving creativity beyond borders...

Let's climb mountain tops of creativity found at valley ebbs of fountain sources,
wing our fears, worries and woes, fly as birds dumping chirping of poetry for service, welcome seeds of genuineness, birthing commitments for better morrow...

Let's build worlds of poetry squares from lines of captured yesterday, Meccas of minds daring today, gardens of herbal thrusts that are boosts of our ancestry

---

Comprising:
For Lagos The Rewind

FESTIVALS OF SHAME

How do we retrace drawn lines of we who said, unlike them, we would fly...bring life to lost swine, offer beats of life to broken hearts, and spaces for stowaways?

How do we inject penned awakening in veins of commonwealth wasters? Unlike them,
hold on as avant-gardes of equity and justice - for humanity's upkeep?

How do we rein in grand-standers of our time and unscrew them off gallery-thinkings of ego-massages fast-drowning our ethos and essence - the foundations for actions, not annual festivals of shame?

Wondering the blaring source of a music whose import of blurriness is fast becoming a sport I mustn't let go, its rhyming weave wraps me direly screwed on my listening caps, compelling a grasp of its calmness, different from the rhythmical "gbam, gbam, gbam" that define us...

Wondering its filtering eeriness, asking if it smells native hands of drumming artistry, contrasting the popular disorderliness ceasing our picture square communities, not letting pages of cultures and traditions, unfold in glee at community squares, not the *"gbimgbimgbim"* that we dance to from ages...

Wondering the place of "ancient and modern" in a modernity sending cultural virtues
On painful flights, the essentials of the 'we that we relegate', the writings of men we neither know nor celebrate, men whose lines should serve drumbeats of

pride and courage in our hearts: NSIBIDI - does it sound like a guitar string?

Wondering if you ever encountered that moment of moments when the sky wondrously rested on waving waves of the sea, the disappearing dance of rainbows, the creative pursuit of setting suns by beings of essence defined by simple lines of creativity - a thrilling consummation of nature....

Wondering if you know the import of your roots and the footages you represent on matters of serious subjects, the facade of your unfolding history, how men are loosing their hoods and hoods of womenfolk are poisoned by a humanity that has lost sense
of direction - oblivious of her needs...

Wondering the source of these dance steps not dancing the songs we sang and claps we clapped at playgrounds of warm communions, steps of jaded souls struggling open mimicry of yesterday but lost its inner depth and souls we should call and speak to
- legends of our ancestry.

THIS POEM...

This poem will spur your day, tear sinuses of disdain and throw up sweet forays to knock down lazing laziness. It will walk paths untamed and strain strains of unwanted pains hung around by planted termites and rain of shame.

This poem was filtered whole-dried-bottled from

seasoned line yards to wet your creative appetites aromatic changes. It was a bold dot tapped free from tree lot of lonely wordings running dotted cravings.

This poem was met at a sparkling corner of genuine unbundling and palpable word-walk felling mines of lined deaths. It's meant to wake up poems saved-healthy in packs of vaults around the world, cocksure-served, whenever.

This poem is a stems'-harbinger on which dreams freely climb - seeding boisterousness and reigns of confidence - a store of poems brought your doorsteps to steer away ineptitudes, wailing attitudes, and latitudes of hanky panky.

Dis poem "na poem wey no common" "Na poem wey carry belle of poems...
Na di kind poem wey go make you want to chop poem like food."
This poem is a unique poem. Dis poem, *naogbonge poem*

I see...

flavours of time sprinkled on rigours of life, generational spurs, stringing parts and piecesof shared bonds, convivial realities strewn on paths of every meet, reverberation of oneness and wings of sweet moments, cohesive essence, sown...an expose of dotted nuisances dancing the golden lanes of humanness, written and seen.

I see...

smiles of genuine outpourings and wondrous depths of

love, showers and cleansers of the handwritings of division, colours of hates and conflicts, greatness of smallness and terrible times of rudderless waste, breeding coinages of retrogression, shared as waters of patriotism, dictates of oligarchic reasoning, vanquishing prized virtues of old.

I see...

that very thought of you boiling in me and us, a collage of greatness, standing value of credibility, rooted sacrifices of pain for gain, comely fragrances of warmness and true bonding of peace reaped, lines of words, and words of hope, rolls of encouragements, and the things we yearn to earn, that moment showed, in brightness of a welcome, flowing the fondness, routing reasons of oneness.

I see...

Comprising:
This Poem I See

DAY OF MY POEMS: MINDING THE CLOCK

This is not another day...

I bring you words that sinkroots seeding paths for tomorrow's greats. None jumps on the fray with a broken pen. Who sits in a cocoon blind-writing the weather? Who sheds light not wearing brightness?

Welcome to a celebration of enduring sauces...crafted as tastes of lasting foods. Who latches on an icing-push not touching the sky? Welcome to worthiness...grab and sip from purpose and focus. Where is the place of our place in climes of places?

This is not another day of no-reckoning where the cunning sits at court. I bring you day of my poems and roads of charted points, minding our clock...reasoned for your use. Who drinks from fountain sources of words bemoaning dearth of words? Who courts analogues e-presenting the future? A celebration of words that run worlds with sense of pride and humility...worlds you can relate. Who learns motor driving with the 'Beatle car', remaining not rugged for life? Welcome to my world of tempting worlds... word scribblers and crafters have their say. What's the fate of them who doubted the sayings of their forebears?

This is not another day...

It's a day of my poems...first written in the language of my people...spoken across the corners and centres of our land. You can't be missing out. I bring you hard foods for thought...eat of them...

As it was in the beginning, do away with broken sentences of inhumanity to man. Why can't we tell it as it is? Why can't we celebrate our culture and the heritage of our art and history to know more about our people and their ways...captured over time? How are heroic ventures made? How do we begin to mind the clock of our world not knowing how bruised we have been? So, let me take you on a ride.

Come with me to the land of my birth, come see mangroves suffer lack of breath, you will encounter magic's of fuels on water, daily fumes caressing our flora and fauna. Come for a feel of everyday stench suffocating the life of our humanity. Come with me to the land of my birth, come see slitting hands of modernity, you will cry for throats of our dear earth raped - on daily-gush of her priceless self to painful wheels of barbarism flown as flag of federalism.

Come with me to the land of my birth, come see the dullness of our waters, you will bemoan its fullness diminished by agents of darkness across our clime. Them, who gleefully wine and dine over waste and wasted souls.

Come for a feel of touching realities, come see how we walk tides of oddities served year-round by heartless hands, air-building today as tomorrow's castles. Those, *thump-chesting* patched feats, rolled our way in disgusting barrows.

Come with me to the land of my birth, where we show-off `sore-sesses' on billboards of shame, also launder-written as spoken words of seriousness - not to be taken as Beats of the Good life.

Come with me to the land of my birth, come see heads spoil for spoils, flirt their farts and draw sketches of coming ceremonies that must hold, in place of next big things that must wait, a celebration of the absence of big pictures.

WALKING BACK TO YESTERDAY AND ROAD TO ZIMBABWE

Welcome to home of the Pen where every line is earned, and reasons are not flukes of seasonal weans, written flights are not might of any dazzling brawn but crafts of tact and brains.

Welcome to homeland of the gods where virtues are worships of passion, eyes are eagles of distant sights, moons of seasonal brightness are celebrations of well-sauced stories.
Welcome to meaning where sense and essence are neither street-dusted, nor cleared of wastes running the drains, gnaws of nameless road traffics and hand writings of unnecessary queues.

Welcome to home of smiling capes dotted by gifts of hanging lakes, footprints of living-dead whose readings are multi-batches of food for generations.
Welcome to waterfalls of poetry - open to eyes that see the seas of life and living - strewn around as muses of nature and nature of open ways of man and purposes they let.

Welcome to the land of living letters, mid-points of earned histories, bravery of drowning merits, extinguishing light for rising power of mediocrity.

Welcome to land of once respected town criers where chests of men are hearts of courage, beaten as drums of war but an extinction to porridge pans of abuses.

Welcome to home of raw tourism visited by them who wondered the depth of civilization never found in their clime, go back to their lines and line them before your children, tell them we are losses that must be won.

Welcome to a walk back to yesterday where words were bonds and hounds were hounded from our communities by words of meaning and power, said by those who speak for the gods.

Welcome to home of the Pen where words are stringed as crafts for generations, hearts of stories are served at village squares with pride and successes were chanted with pomp to the heavens.

I know a place called Zimbabwe. Let's cool off a bit. Let's go to Zimbabwe where questions wag between fun and merriment.

Where were you when our pockets pointed fishes for kill in makeshift rivers and conviviality smoke alive from barbeques? Where were you, when BLAKES was face of entertainment in town and CARAMELO was one-man band stand?

Where were you when the Naira had teeth and Sixty Naira was all you needed to taxi-drop your way in the city centre? Where were you when the language of unity wasn't paper large without a voice but choice with a united poise?

Where were you when pipe-born waters whistle-cry freedom from surplus pipes serving homes of fewer residents? Where were you when rush to this city birthed marriages of convenience and homes had their knees maimed for life?

Where were you when boredom of city centre, One man Village, Nyanya, Mararaba, converge on ZIMBABWE?

BLOCKADES AND ACCOLADES: SOUNDS AND CATWALKS

How do I write you my heart's bottom of secret deaths I died not telling? How it's been a world of amazement walking in my head?

How do I bring you feelings of my dearest longings for the meaning of you who hold aloft as flag of flying aces?

How do I speak of my world of jaded un-reckoning - made whole, hungering for difference in unimaginable writes?

How do I begin to roll back a world load of stubborn ignorance whose confidence is a school many should attend?

The Hows and the Whys, the Ups and the Downs, the stakes and the plaques, Blockades and Accolades, the today of yesterday?

How do I tell fits of telling fits and starts? The starting lines of bottom lines, top down and bottom up and luck of level bottom starts?

Who tells the fitness of given literary profoundness not taken through funnels of life and daily engagements?

On the day courage was summoned, you opened as a page of nature and overflow of essence for a better tomorrow.

On the day you wriggled before my face, your cat-walking sounds were handed as lines for a book, alerting reminders of you.

On the day your smile rubbed on me, i touched the finest of art I ever yearned to read and the fullness of happenstances beyond man.

On the day a world slipped your gap-toothed window, wishes and horses met at a world of equilibrium where forever gifts converge.

If courage is man, I toast to me who braved your serenity and captured the beauty of catwalks, in unforgettable lines. Lines firing me till date.

I no dey like pretending...I only dey see di ending... and I know sey, you no know sey your fire dey catch for my body. Even with all your forming, I dey see nothing but one thing. Because me sef know sey, anyhow things dey, one day be one day water go pour for my body.

I no mind your wetin be wetin. Your vex dey tell me one thing; to keep to dey tell you sey, na only you I still dey see sey, go fit be wetin be di wetin, wey go quench dis fire for

my body.
Now, I have some searching questions for you:

When I walk the corridors of your world, what warms to you as lines you can vouch?

When I come face to face with your face, what would your space create as our place?

What's the distance between the days of yore and prancing hands of today's digital cores?

Won't you rather fly to trekking your lines? What's your place in poetry to screens?
When you walk the sentences of my senses, what do you hope to reap in every sense?

If questions are not questions in all for good, won't some die never raised as questions?
Can we for a moment question the question of our togetherness? How did we get here?

I know we are forever hooked but:
Would you bring down the roof's top as proof of our growing union? Would you pump your cries in decibels warm and let the corners of my ears enjoy the strengthening feel of her moans, awaiting sky drops of living waters, telling how earthly spirits commune in heavens on earth?

Would you spin words of soothing kills as proof of the skills you pride? Would you screw them for lasting impacts and let your every move be a spice-full statement of your worthy craft and smooth capacity to string smiles from sheer nothing? Would you show stuff you are made, while making bangs of cupful creams?

Get to the beginning of the starting as you write the steps taken at starting and toiling walks of leg-walking, roads plied whilst honing what's what and what's not, in matters of the heart, weakened and strengthened by waving waves - of moods, temptations, temperaments, the musical notes of crying moments and times of smiling pockets.

Let's walk to the bank of river "Ingerin" whose lively grins smack the green of our common desire, what we mean to every eye that sees our steps, not our veins hankering to that bell ringing us-joined - sharing shelters of flying whistles, pencilling life and erasing hiccups; flipping pages, forever hooked.

Comprising:
1). Blockades and Accolades
(2) Sounds and Catwalks
(3) Dis fire
(4) Questions
(5) Forever hooked.

COLLAGE OF THOUGHTS

Thoughts of you do dominate my space with burning urge to paint you maps of enlivening things we said when age didn't see today, they sit large in their worlds, spewing mucking sounds of discouragement, attempts at weathering their ways land at blocks, but flashbacks let a natural flow that sets one's recesses with inspirational empowerment for a strangulation of the one named procrastination, never have I associated with it, it dreads me, I damn it, some say; it killed their dreams, others worship it, saying; it's a muse that must be placated. o! Not me who stands on its head, drumming lines, of careful crafts, because everything and everywhere hold creative charges. I take liberty of freedom, freedom to create and recreate broken bones and battered hopes.

Thoughts of you are showers of memories that come handy at mattered times, when my world reaches for a replay of telling episodes, the Bermudas of our world, nosediving climes and unfathomable mazes; throats of our bones and Romes that would never be built - how they dawned yesterday as promises of today - bungled our 'morows, today's dwarfs in high places, the insane that speaks focus for the sane and blots miles covered in all, not what we knew or may never know, nor history of evil conspirators, not national carriers grounded in foreign vaults nor rivers polluted by killing hands of death, not desert games wasting souls by the day nor oases of life snuffed underground, not lost magic nor pyramids of credibility and hard work beaten blue into tiny spaces of mediocrity, warped thinking and flight of national consciousness.

No! No! Not what we bargained. Not the writings we read

when the union flag was hoisted amid voices of hope, echoed by our masters. Not the one that recaptured our moods, feelings and hopes but mouth-rendered for its sake - never going past throats. No! Not the machinations of deadened consciences pocketing our collective till. Not the one holding the mic, bestriding a stage - sick from the workings of a backstage; empty of finesse and ingredients for holistic deliveries. These thoughts bug me night and day. Your worries are my worries that roll aloud on the grounds of an ailing polity. So, I bring you words of how your thoughts, are daily inspirations that collapse in mine and how they boldly say...we are going down, the stage is empty...calling a rescue.

IF YOU SHOULD KNOW ME: RETURN OF PYRAMIDS

Someone feels he/she is too weird to be your friend but in innocence and ignorance, you keep pushing for him/her. He/she looks at you and says; if you should know me...
Someone feels he/she should be sitting on your head sipping his/her wine, but you are going all out to get him/her from the woods, he/she says; if you should know me..."
Someone completely drenched from a sudden rain was offered a ride but he/she thinks you don't deserve a car and says; *na me supposedey drive dis motor...*

I bring you a brand of bread, simply spread thin threads of onions and freshly cut pepper of Nigerian descent, and see if waters won't grace your eyes, as you sing songs of way back days when as children, we dug in sand and cooked soups, never tasted.

I bring you stories of broken pancakes and rounded *kpofkpof,* survivors of generations of Dislikes, holding on as snacks of pride served in names of flying colours - shared as flour worlds of love in little ways that matter.

Bring on your pen-rifles, be unruffled by wailing ways threatening minds and letters. Let's replay tons of forgotten ease and position humility's place in all. Let's keep our streets running on themes of virtuosity.

If bread and kpofkpof are blessings and *guguru and granut* still sing singles, it is possible that our dearest okpa would play snack of choice in bowels of flying birds. We can turn back the clock's hand and raise pyramids of grounded nuts that stood us heads and shoulders high as pride of a nation.

Certainly, this is my poetry...A taste of the following would blow your mind but let's spice some pleasing calm...

Someone said his heart syncs with my lines of poetry that each time she read me, she crumbled in shredded tears, but when asked if he would mind a taste of a freshly baked one, he smiled saying she is always cool - with my poetry.

Someone turned blind eye at my lines saying, she would go for only hardcore ones written in pidgin. When note of enquiry was scribbled her way, she said soft lines of ice cream and packs of dodo pizza won't bring the magic of hard core poetry - my poetry.
He could be fickle-minded when hardness should reign but she would go for him saying; he comes in colours of bliss. How he drives home his points is a point of note and many die for a dive...a nuisance of sort - yes, she said so but holds

on like bee to honey - to my poetry.

She is the nicest one in the universe with hearty smiles of golden beholden - he is the vase of her flowering glow... often, she is branded in his colours that set others wondering how they bond, where they sowed their seed of beginning and the depth of lines they fly - it's not his poetry - it's my poetry.
Someone said she will build me castles of landmines if she don't read him a poem tonight, this night of many nights when she direly needed a hug full of poems but he loathed my poetry - he called for Shakespearean classics - she can't do without local flavours of poetry, my poetry... he fell for my poetry. I know you have fallen for my poetry - my poetry.

Comprising: *If you should know me *Return of Pyramids *My Poetry

=Part Two B=

THE SPOKEN CALL

(NAIJA PIDGIN)

IF SEY I BE SPOKEN WORD POET

If sey I be spoken word poet, I go use pidgin write statements wey heaven go welcome, use words build houses weypipul go stay, be di truth wey Ifeanyi Bernard represent, do fast-forward poetry performance of McNaevets, join di boat of Dike Chukwumerije and swim for rivers of credibility, use poetry talk to pipul and government to hear di openness of transparency and good governance.

If sey I be spoken word poet, I go beat my drum, shake my shekere and dance my poetry like Evelyn D'Poet, use di stage with confidence of Solutionist Clementina, craft mountains of solutions from fountains of knowledge, make meanings from everything, see any stage performance as something wey I no go tek play.

If sey I be spoken word poet, I no go do poetry for poetry sake for my pocket, I go pocket my shoulder for inside pockets of life, tell di world sey, di gift of poetry na for society, na for pipul to see di difference between progress and development and tell how lie-lie dey put wedge for our tomorrow, bring out the colours of poetry and tell pipulsey, di white, blue or black of poetry, no mean sey no be one poetry, I go hang the signboard one poetry, one humanity without shaking.

If sey I be spoken word poet, I no go fail to recognise di place of Oral tradition, I go promote di tongues of poetry, I go let pipul know where we dey come from, I go tell how come no fit be kom, I go yan how we don become pipulwey don dey lost for wilderness of shame, I go bring our matter to di table of matters, talk why we be wetin be now, and that nawetin we use our hands cause. And if where we wan be deh important, we must take oursef with seriousness.

If sey I be spoken word poet, I go tek poetry enter di moon, but I go follow Charity start from home, I go climb di mountains of Wushapa, drink di water of Iyake Lake for Ado-Awaye - di only hanging lake for our kontri, I go tek poetry to the water goddess of Ekogbene for Delta and perform poetry for where salt water and fresh water meet, I go stand on top of Mambilla plateau, and tell pipulseyMambilla and Obuduna pride of our nation, I no go make mistake to siddondey do poetry for inside one big box because, outside di box big pass everything for inside the box.

If sey I be spoken word poet, I go box my way dey go with poetry of colours, I go tek my pidgin crack coconut for Badagry and drink garri like sey tomorrow no dey for Calabar, I go tek one hand hold Mic deyyan and di other go dey play with amala and abula, I go tell my fellow poets sey, voice wey go sharp, need correct Naija pepper, I no go form sey text book food na di matter, I go bring customers come Mama Put for every area because, from time to time, I go dey do street poetry and take di fight for better living to di corners of our community, I go let our pipul know di kind sun weydey burn us and wetin we fit become if we dey do di right things. I go tell everybody sey, everywhere nastage for poetry but poetry wey speak for di pipul, pass all stage about poetry put together – poetry na life.

Written in Naija pidgin

Part Three

BONUS READ

Two Kids

I speak in letters of lines you can feel
I run lines of bold realities
I seek moulds of hard cores reeling
In smoking facts of life.
I crave hands of fitting uplift
For a people deep in self-wrought.
I steal the lines of old and new
Raising pillars yearning
Gainful today and tomorrow.
I draft crafts of lasting memories
Drawn from wells of yesterday's
Bards and grey-haired ones, in tune
With gauging and staging virtues for good.

I speak in lines of letters you can relate
Unbundling rots cutting holes of death
In wailing pockets across our space
Whilst planting sores of pain and sorrow.
I roam hearts around the world for hopes
Battered dry by bulldozers and caterpillars.
I dig deep for period finds from the youth
Holding ropes railing into tomorrow.
I sing in tongues unloading
Real crafts minted for all
And conscience mortgagers
Parading streets of gods
For hero-worships

I speak from the skies of Europe
Across the rising dew of Bosphorus.
Today is Children Day in Turkey
Kids are gifted packages for being kids
Celebrated in the bowel of a Turkish bird
Faraway deep in the skies, nearby.
Seated by are two Nigerian kids
Smiling lovely smiles of hope
Only made real by patriotism
Rubbished by Corruption
Back home, headed.
Two kids...What hope?

For good...

That place and time came
Without a click, rolling back the
Innocence of our sincerity
Enveloping us till date.
The gate opened onto the road
For a meeting of two;
strange brother
And sister...blind to colour,
creed and more.

That day, that meet of auras
Convivial yesterday till date
Beauty...from the inside
Never weather beaten.
Turn back the hand
Of our thoughts...tell me

Clicking sounds...

Take a deep breath
Tell me; we are not
brother and sister.
These lines are for you...
yes...for us
Who read them long before
Lettered bold on that cake
you baked me
When I knew cakes not.
In return, I bake you these lines
Eat them in remembrance of
The love bathed...before
Wrapped in the arms
Of forever yours.

www.ingramcontent.com/pod-product-compliance
Lightning Source LLC
LaVergne TN
LVHW090137160826
845673LV00017B/2497

* 9 7 8 9 7 8 5 8 1 1 3 3 9 *